Color Me Calm

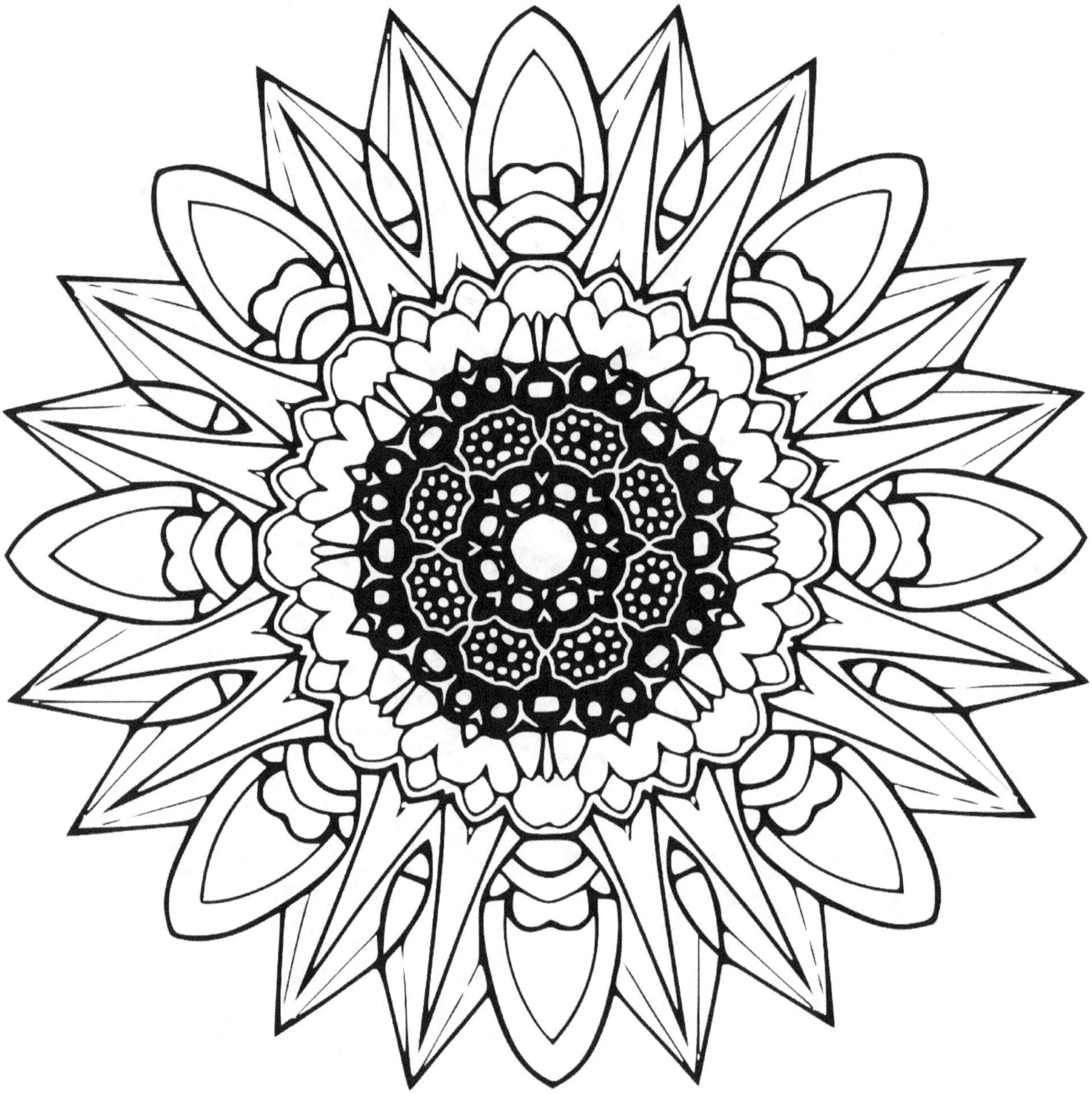

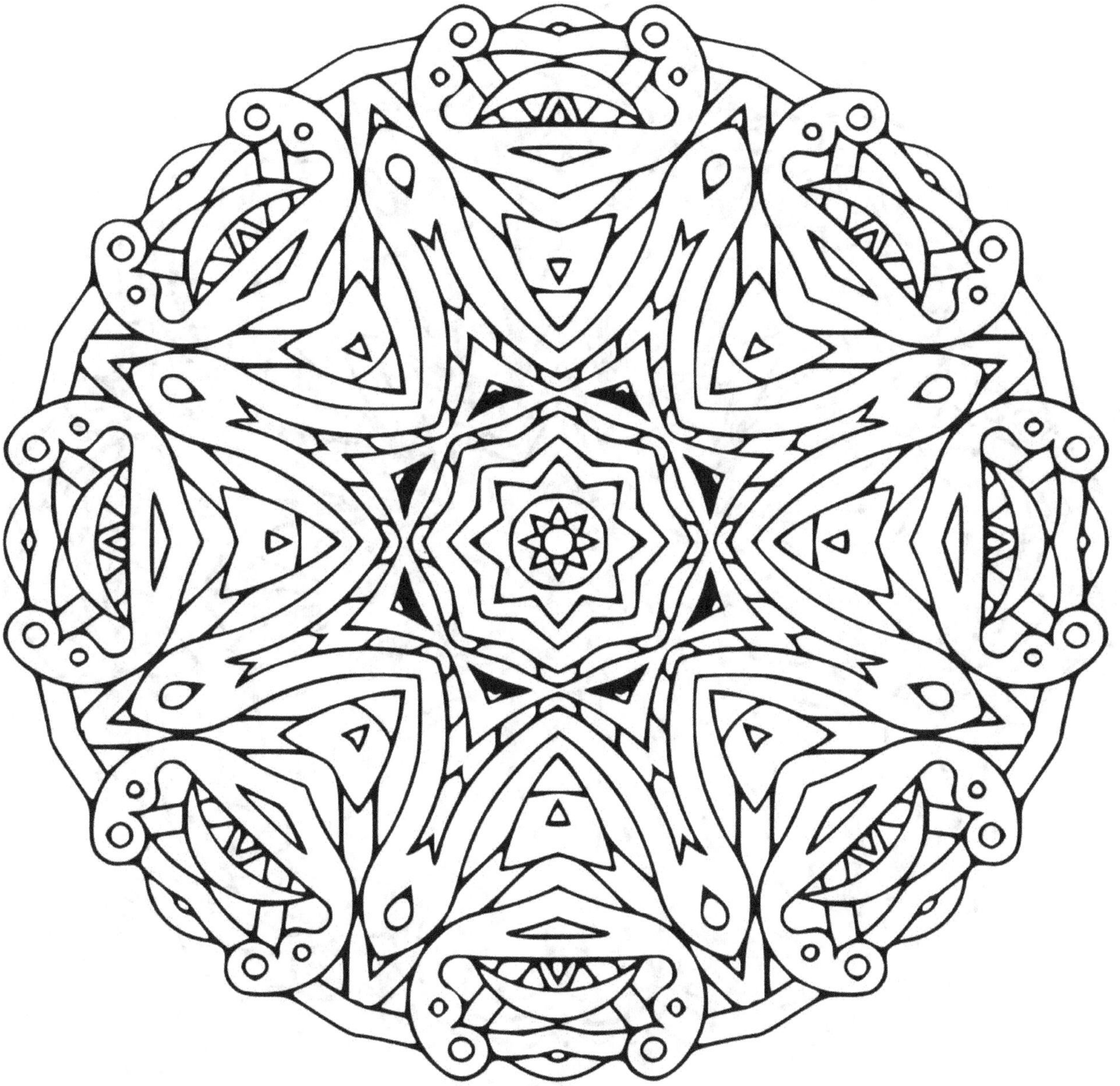

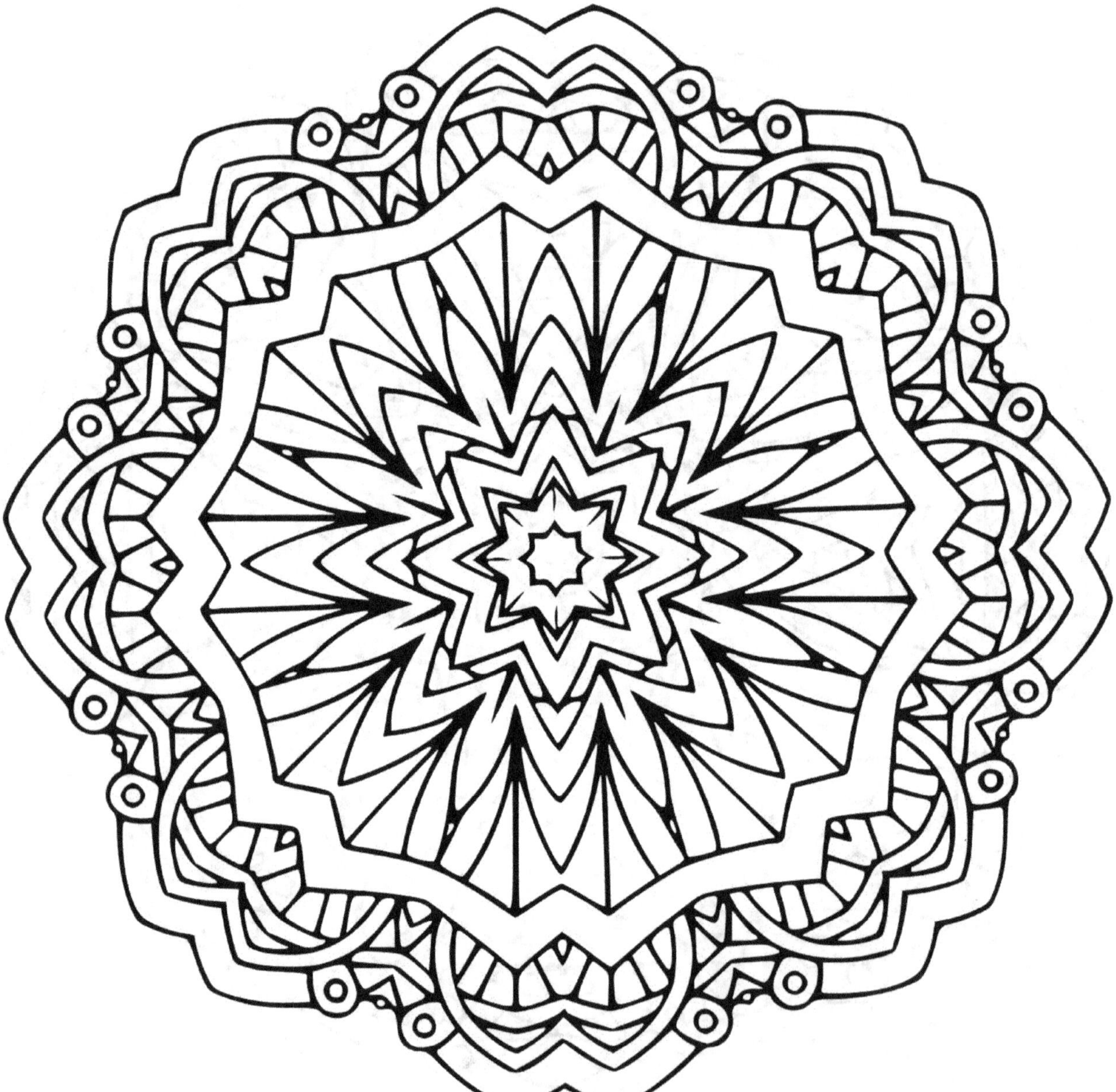

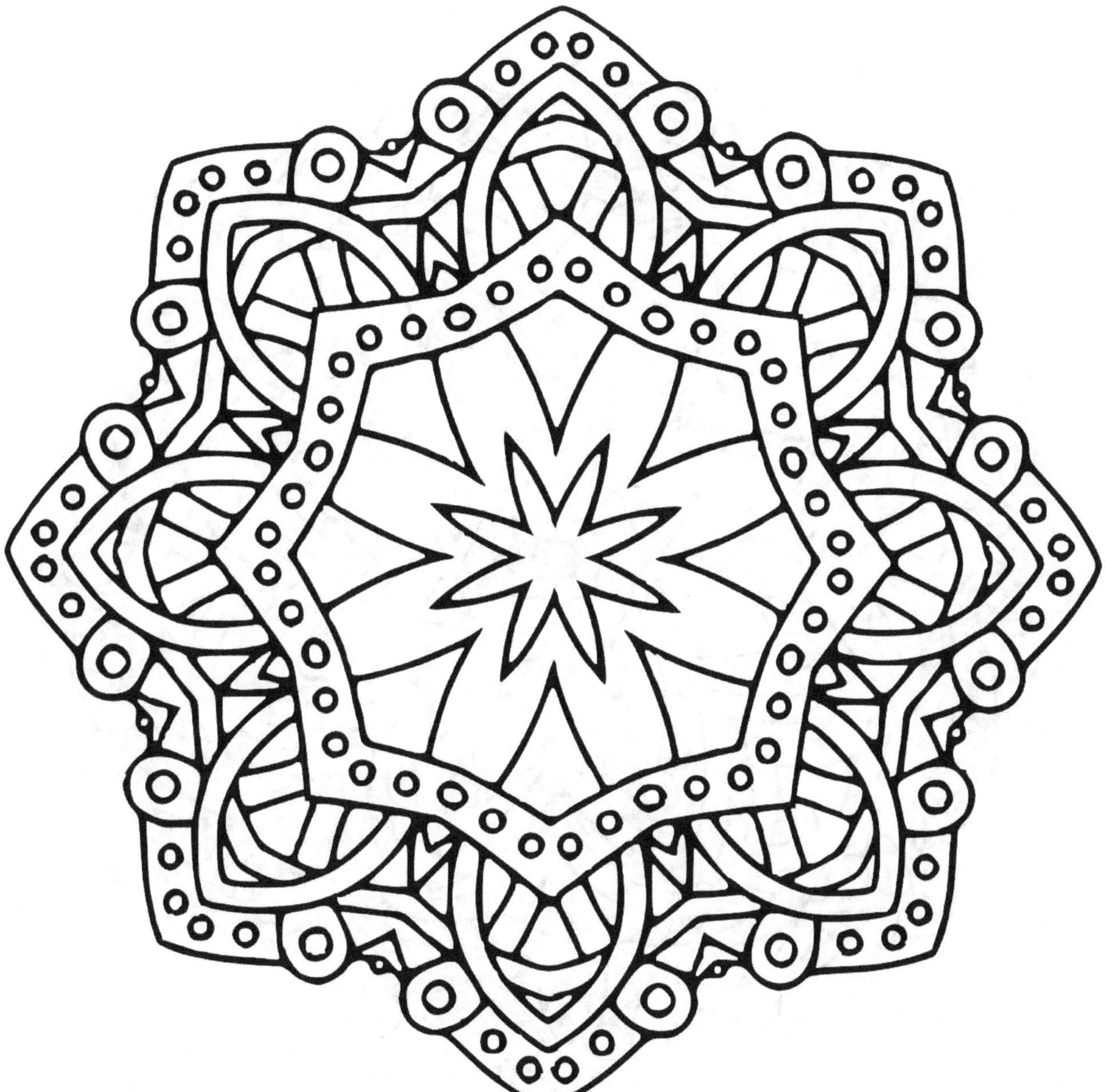

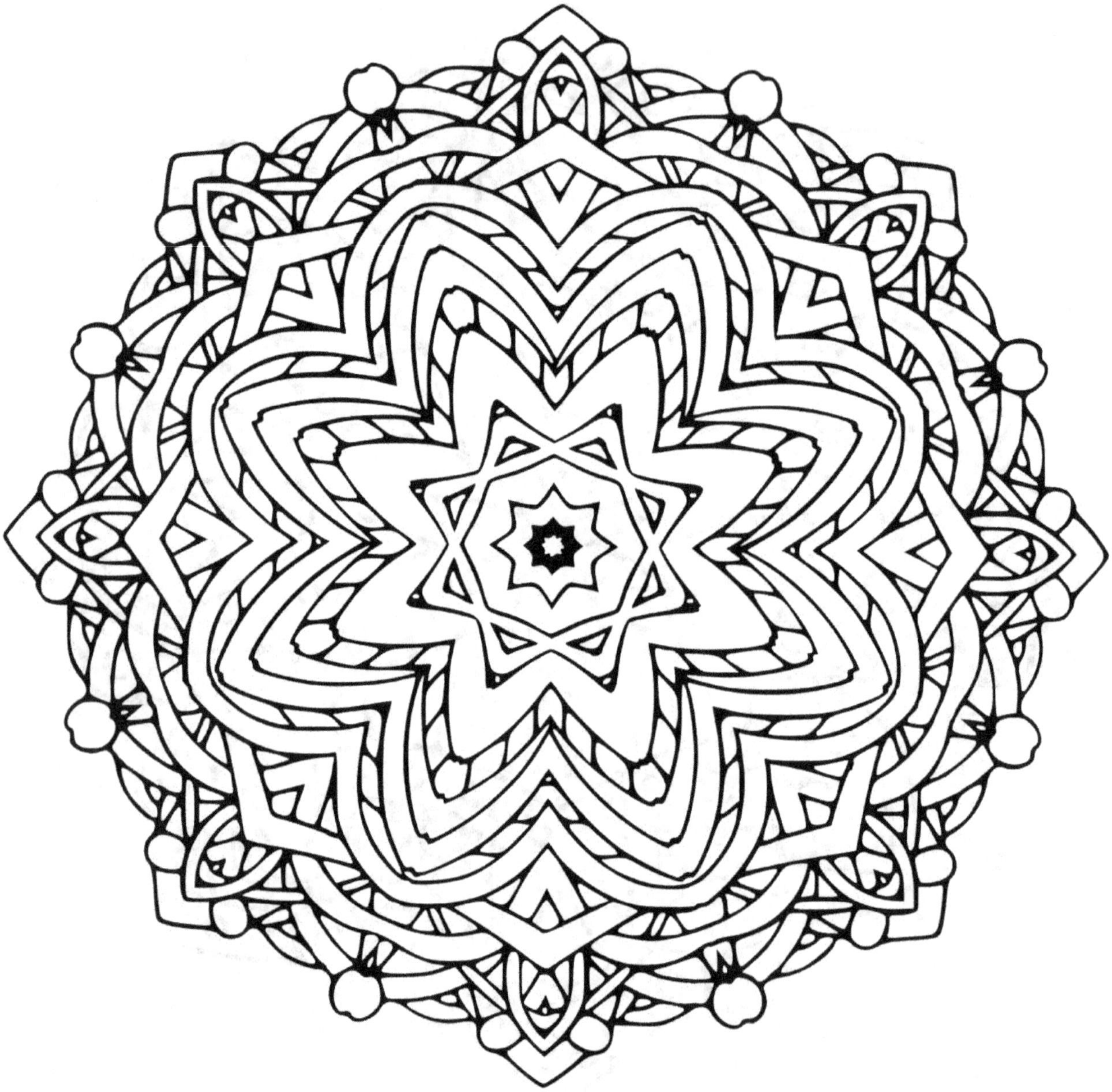

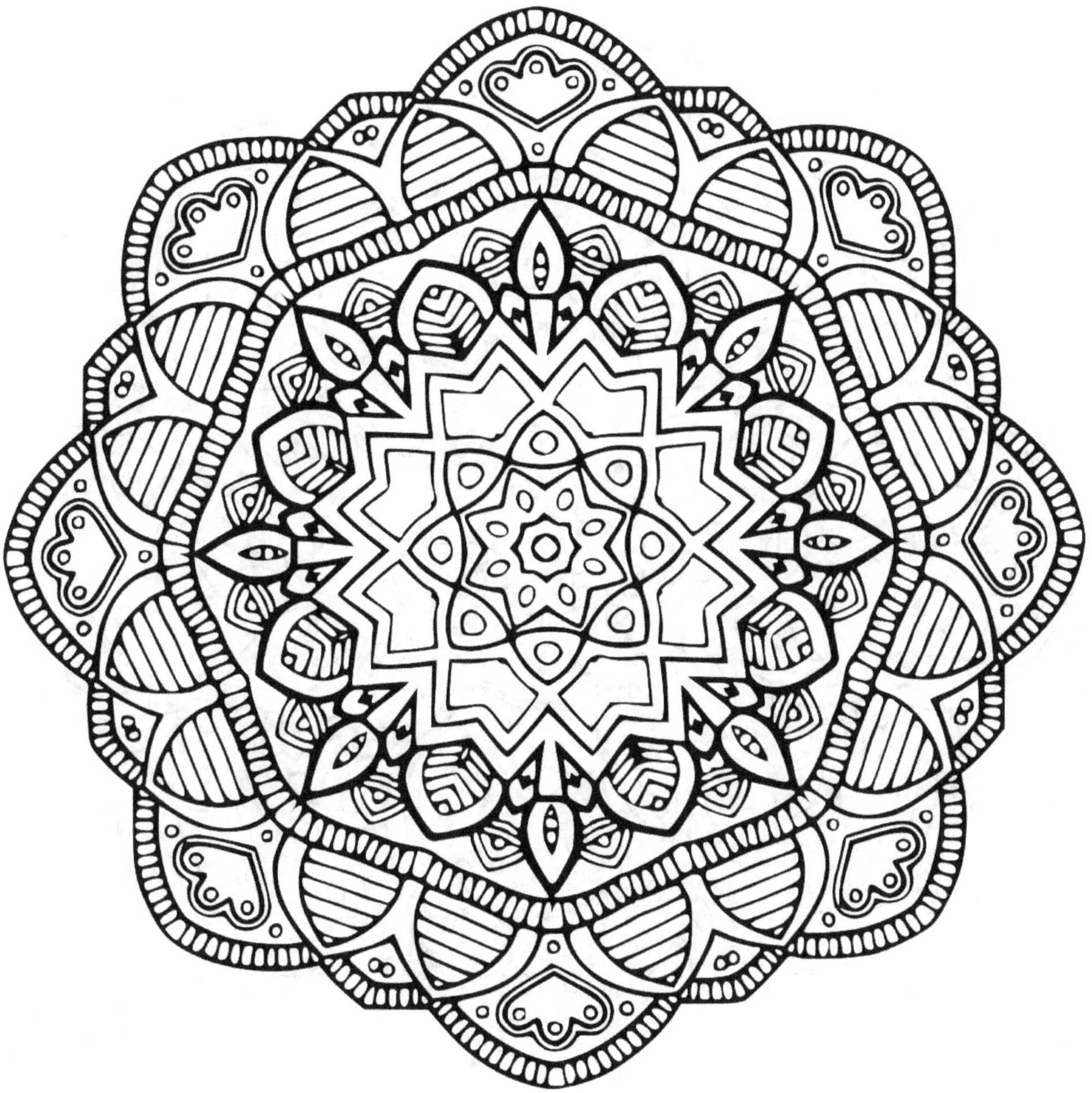

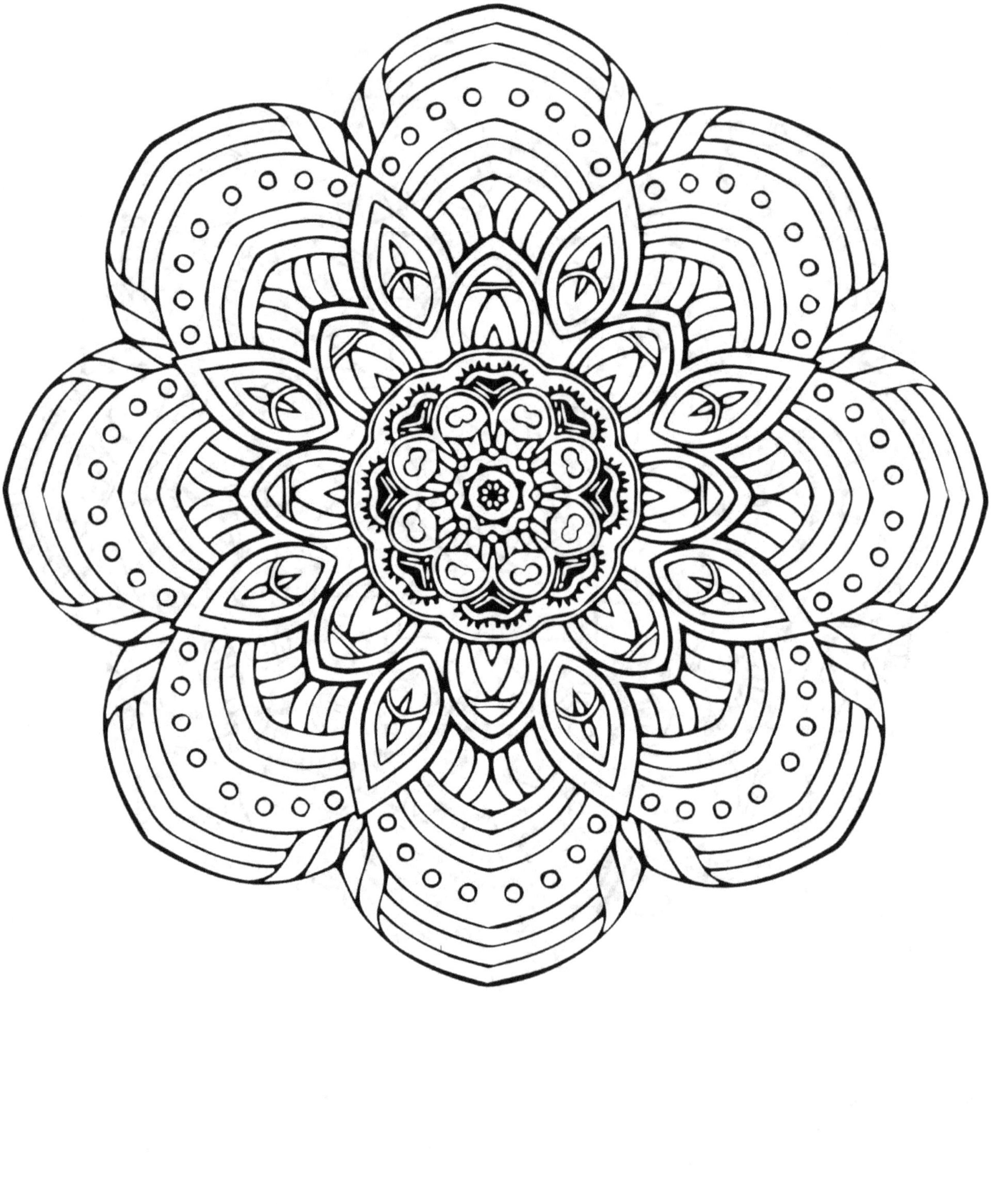

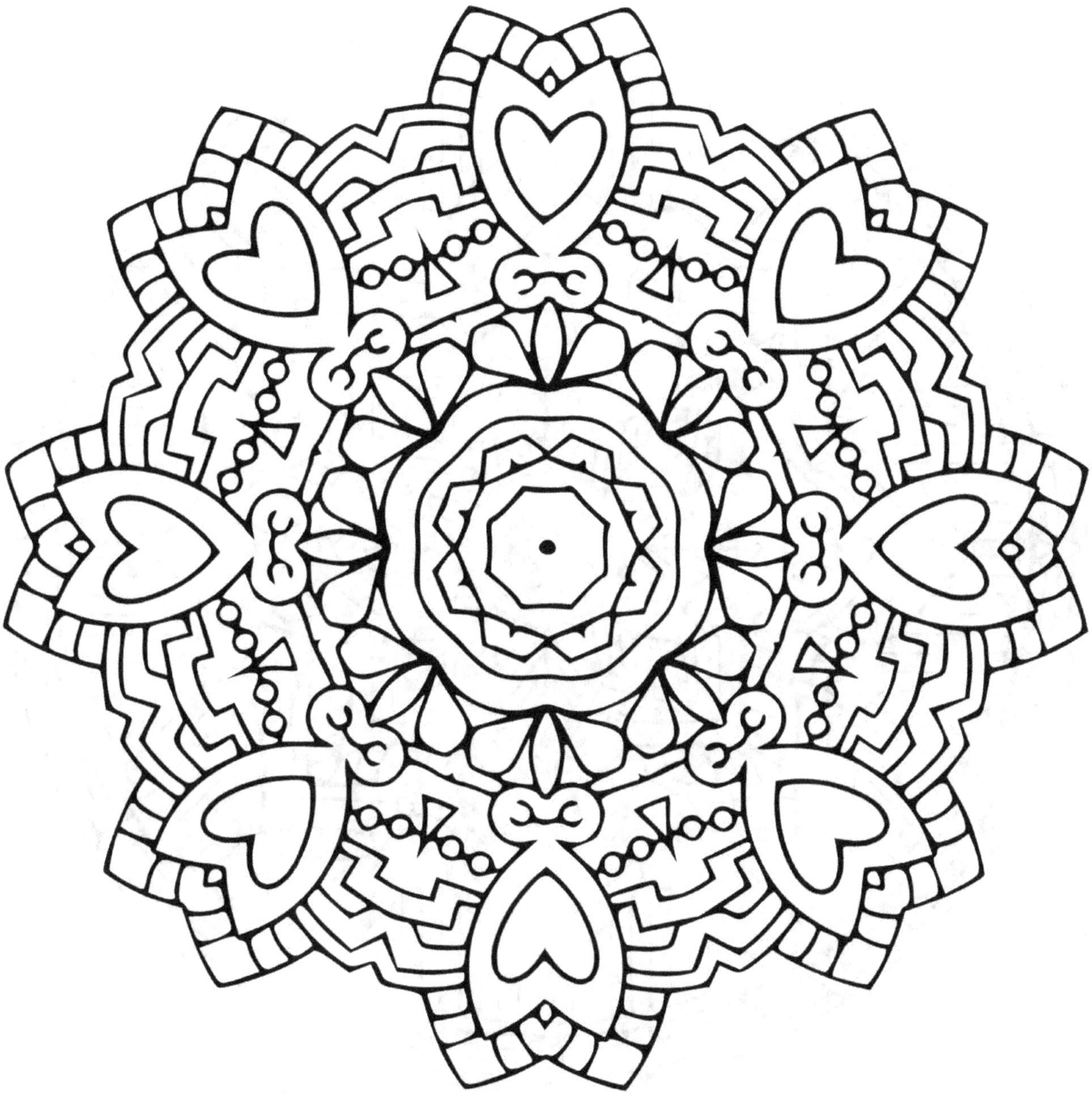

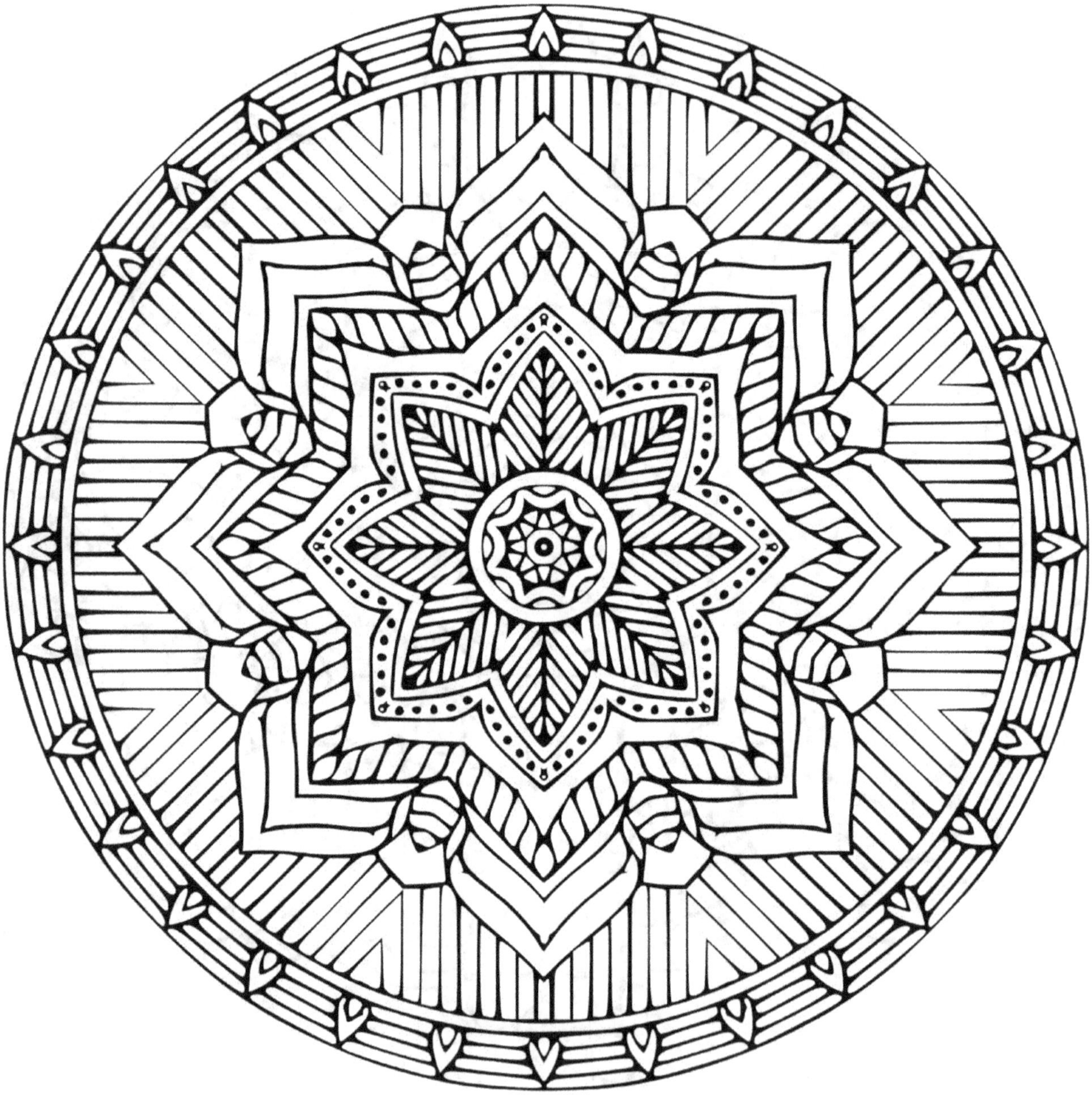

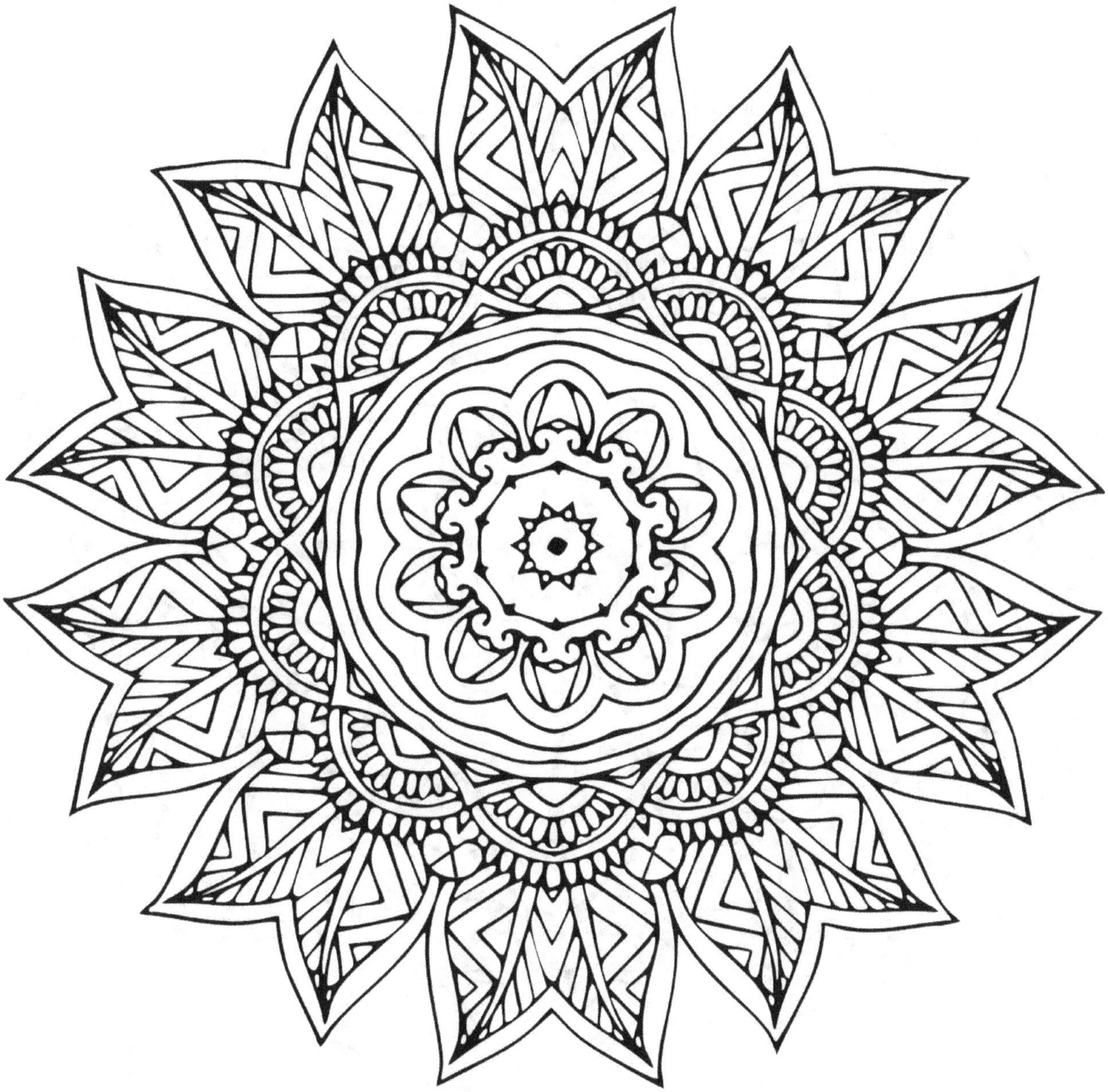

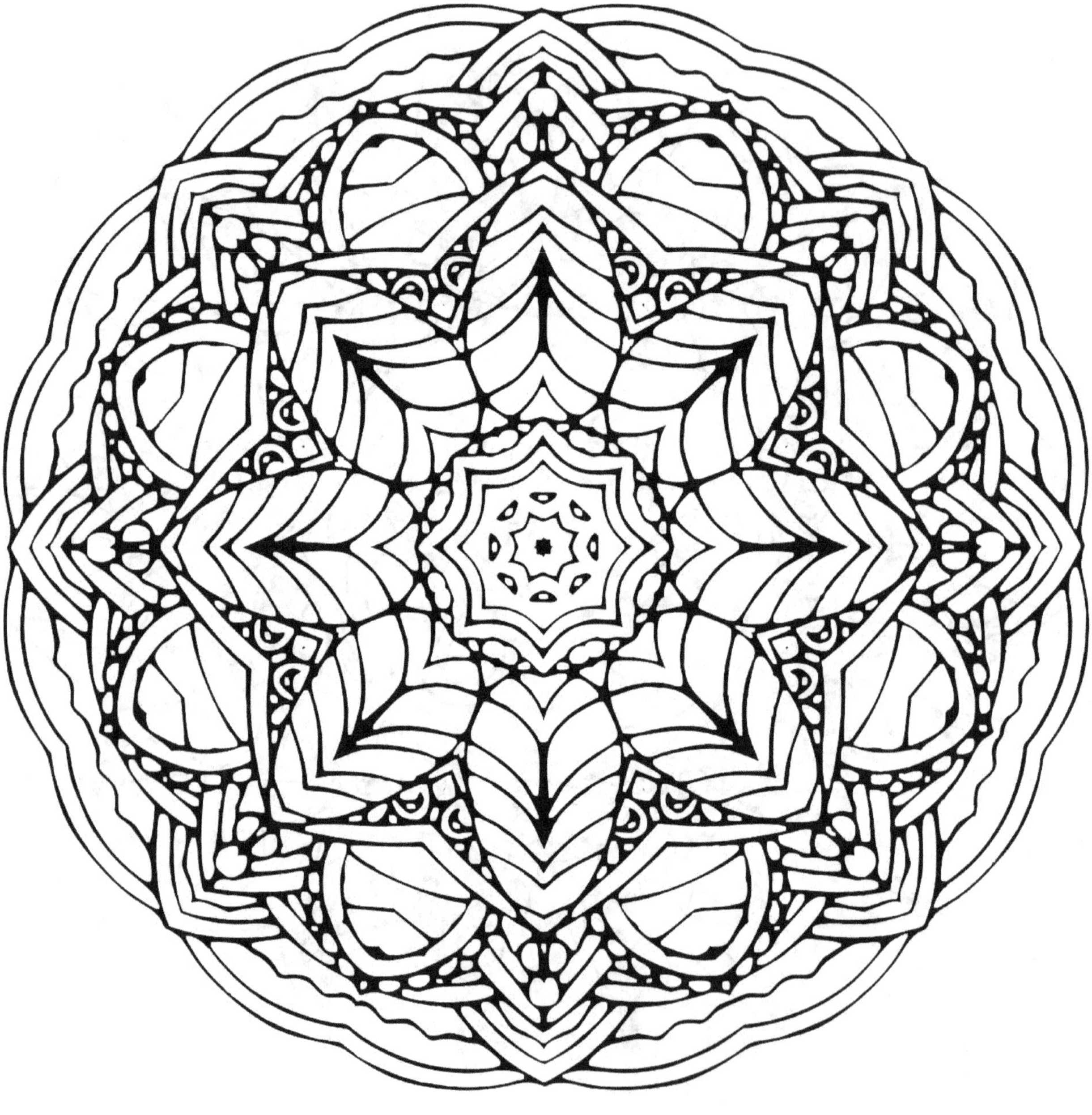

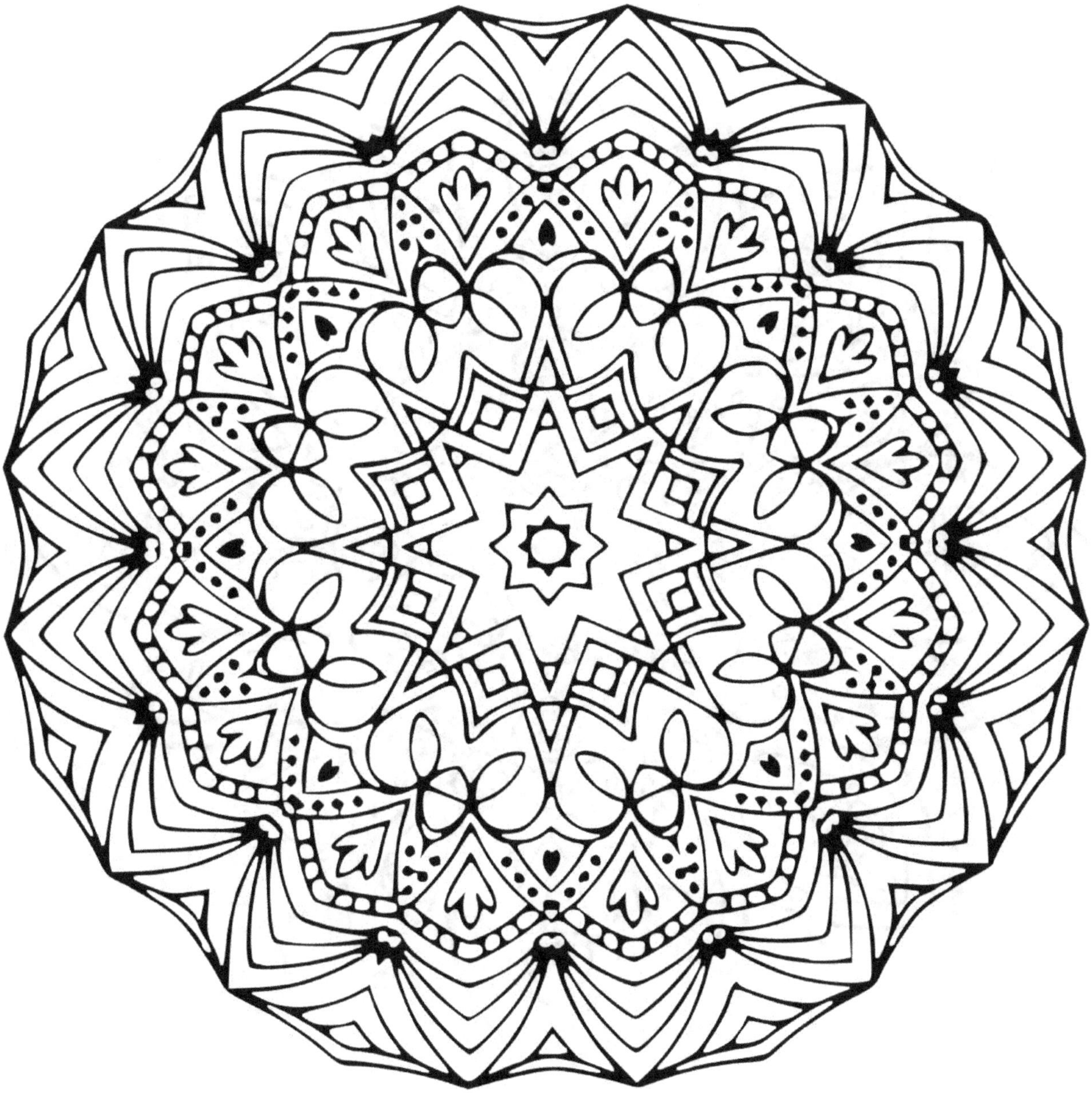

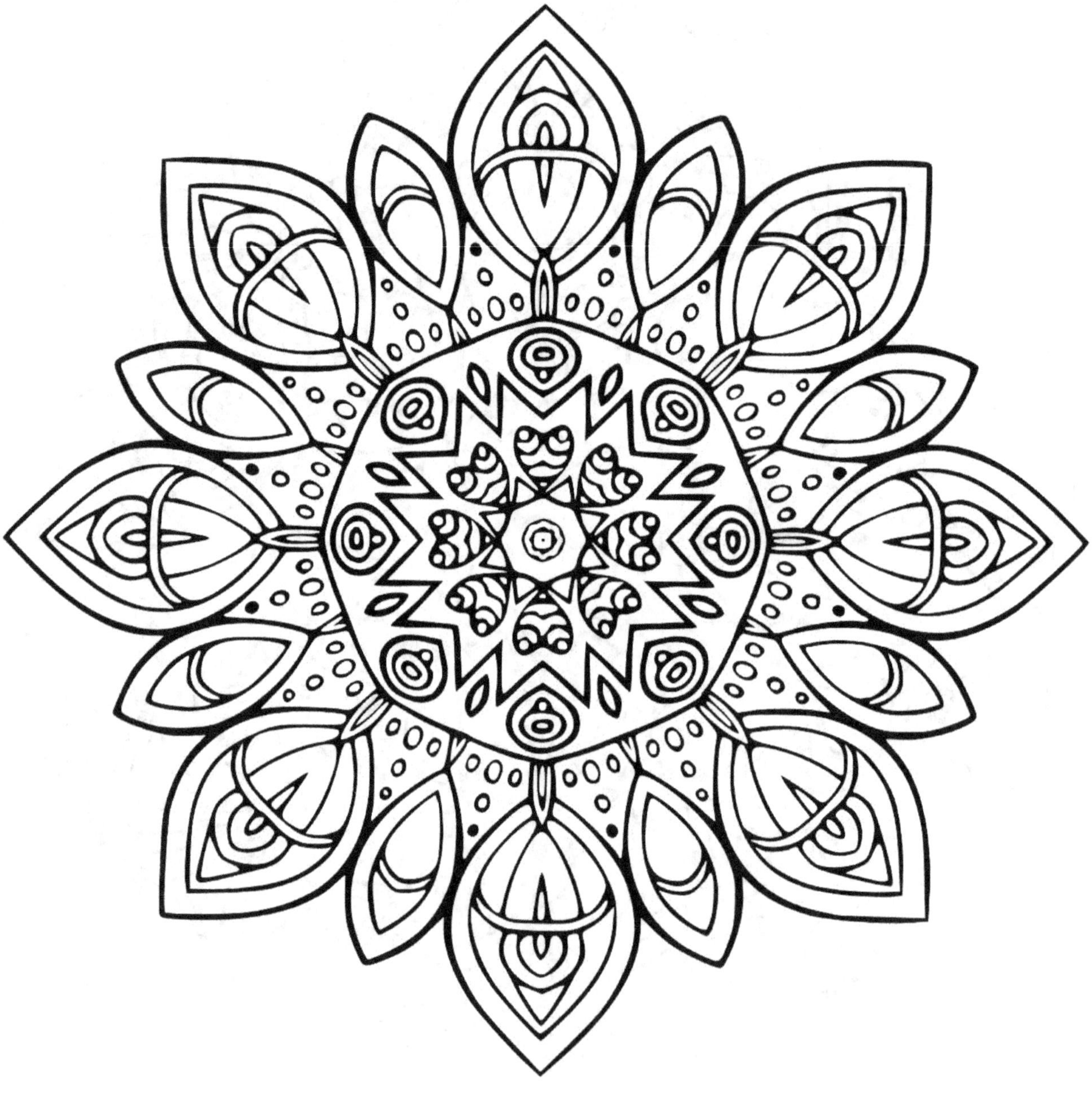

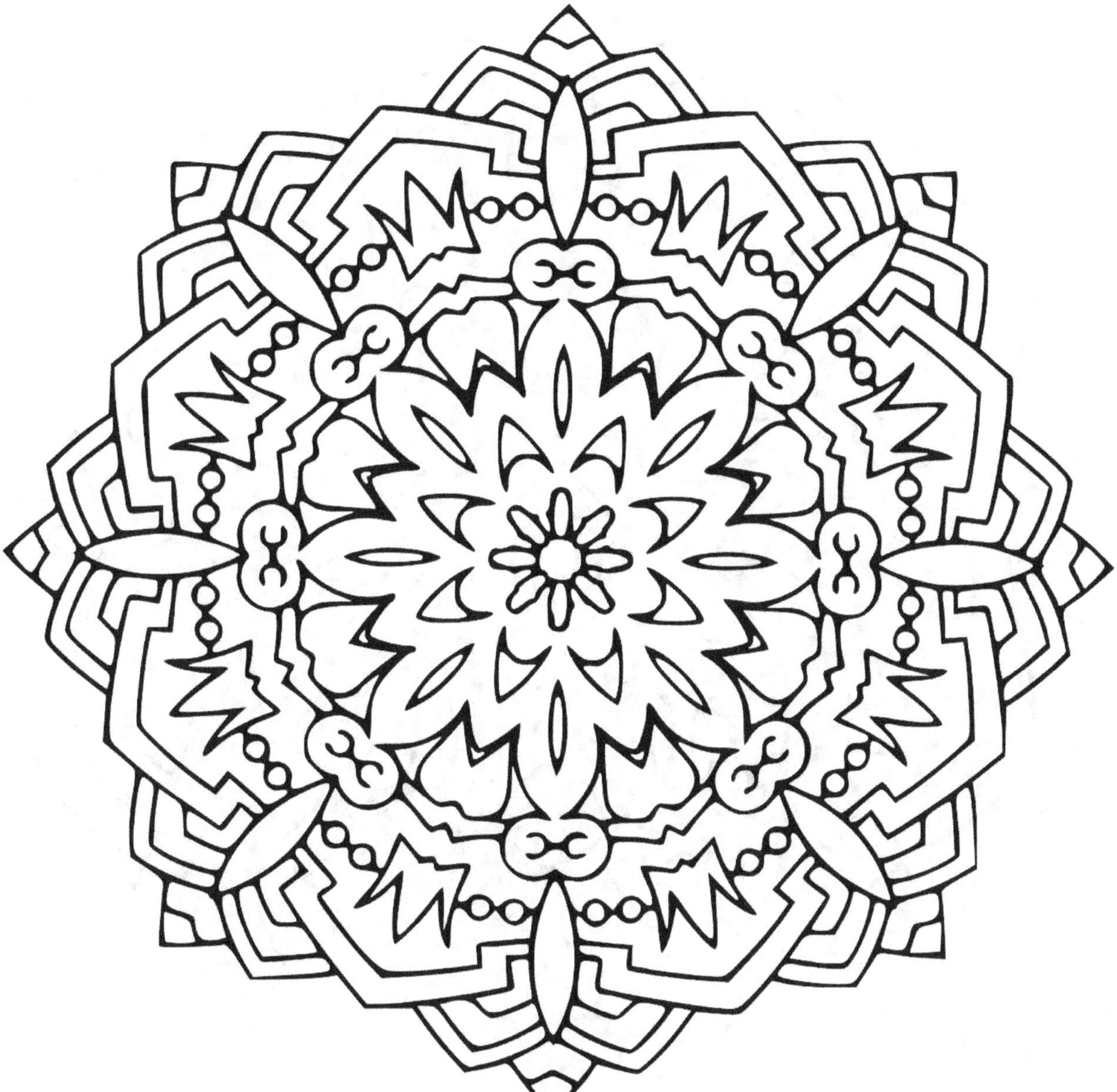

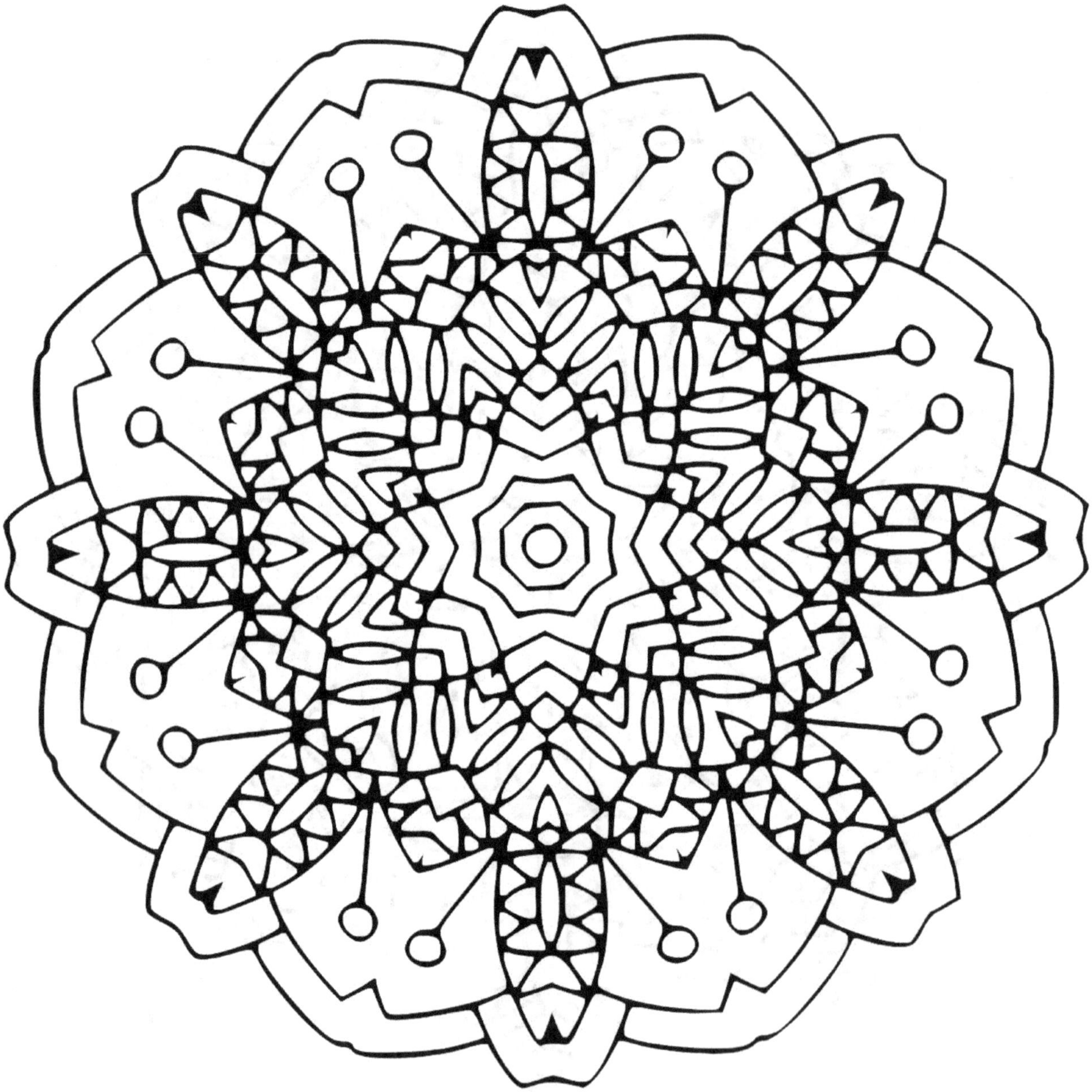

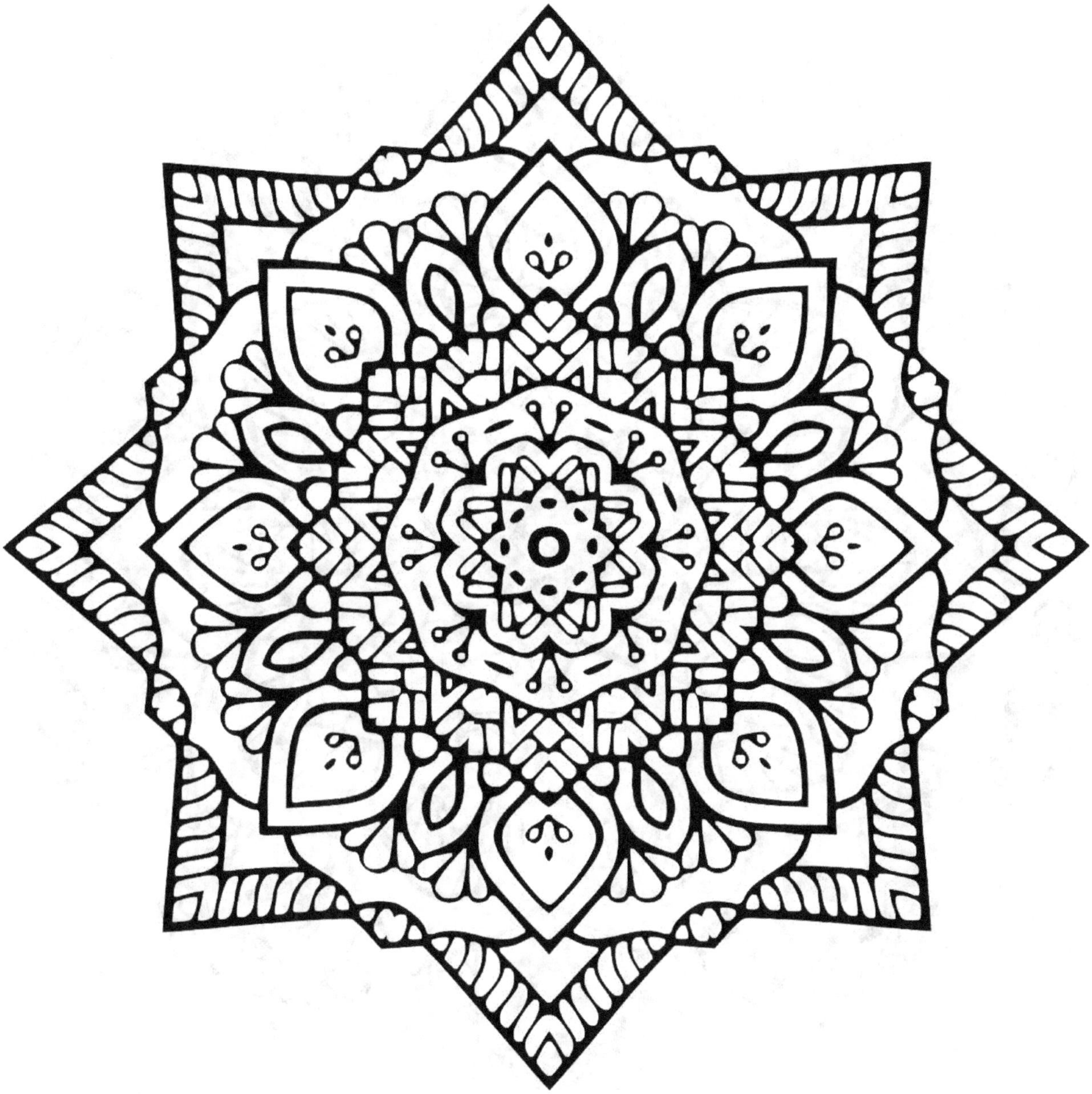

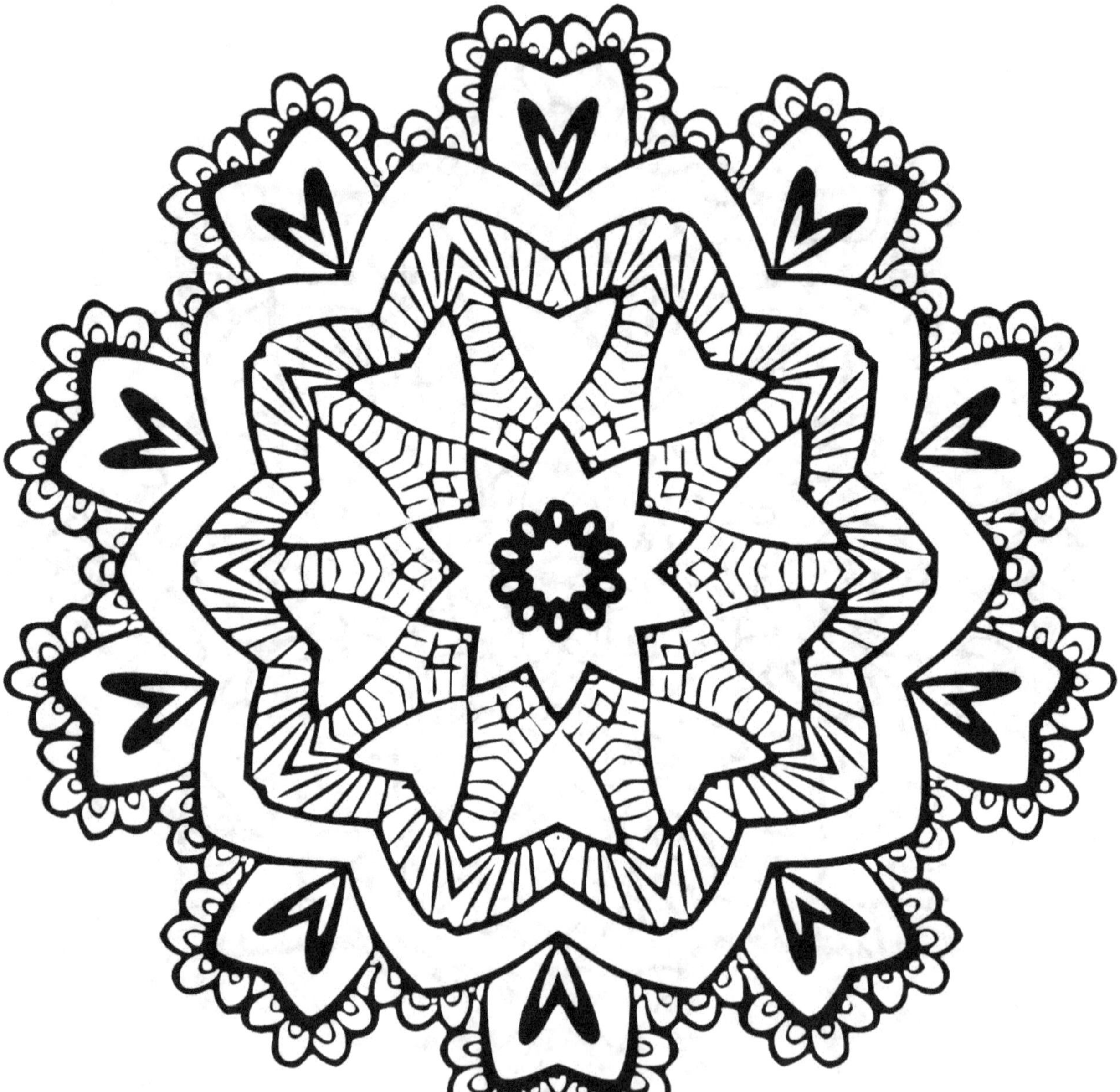

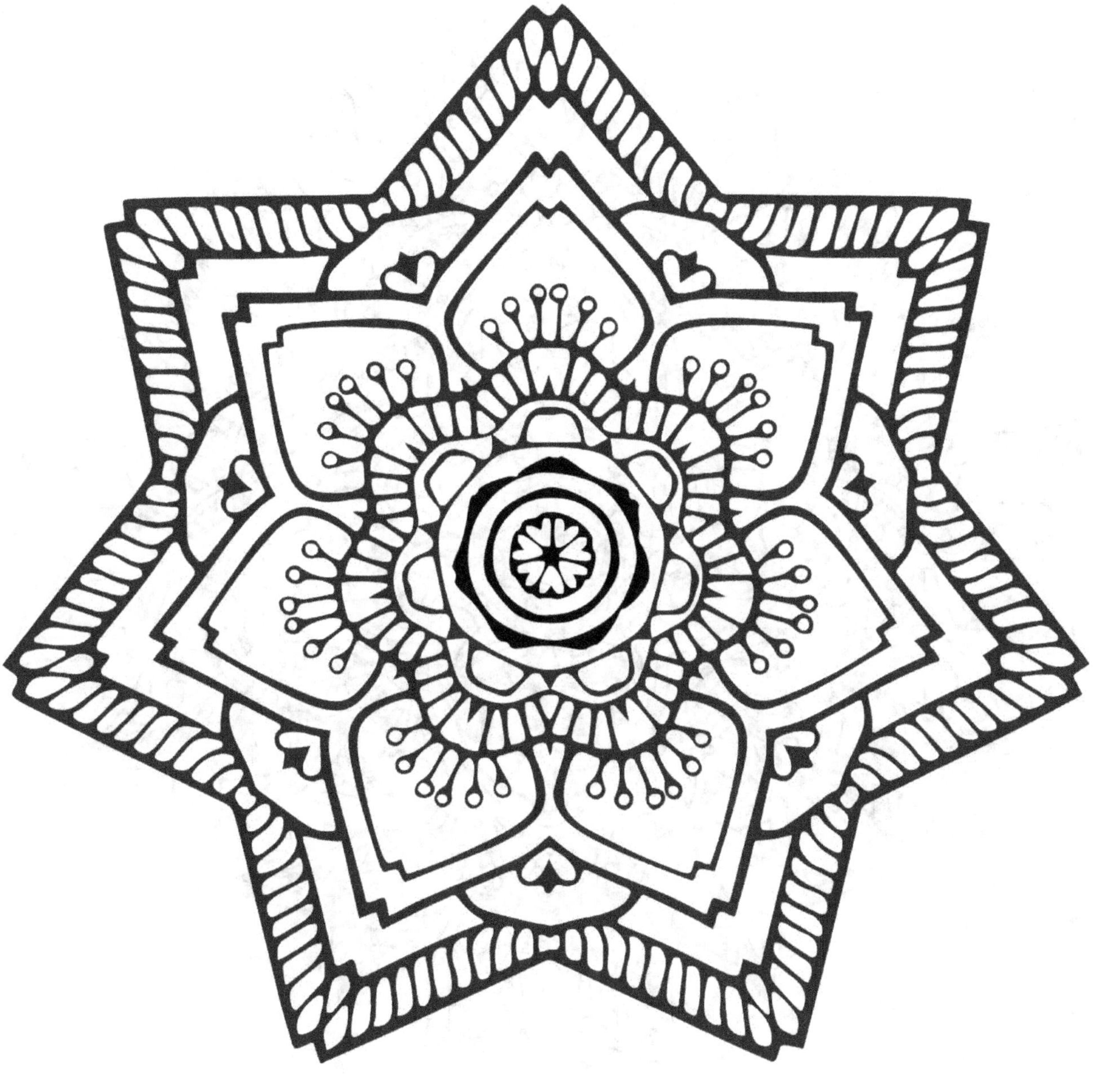

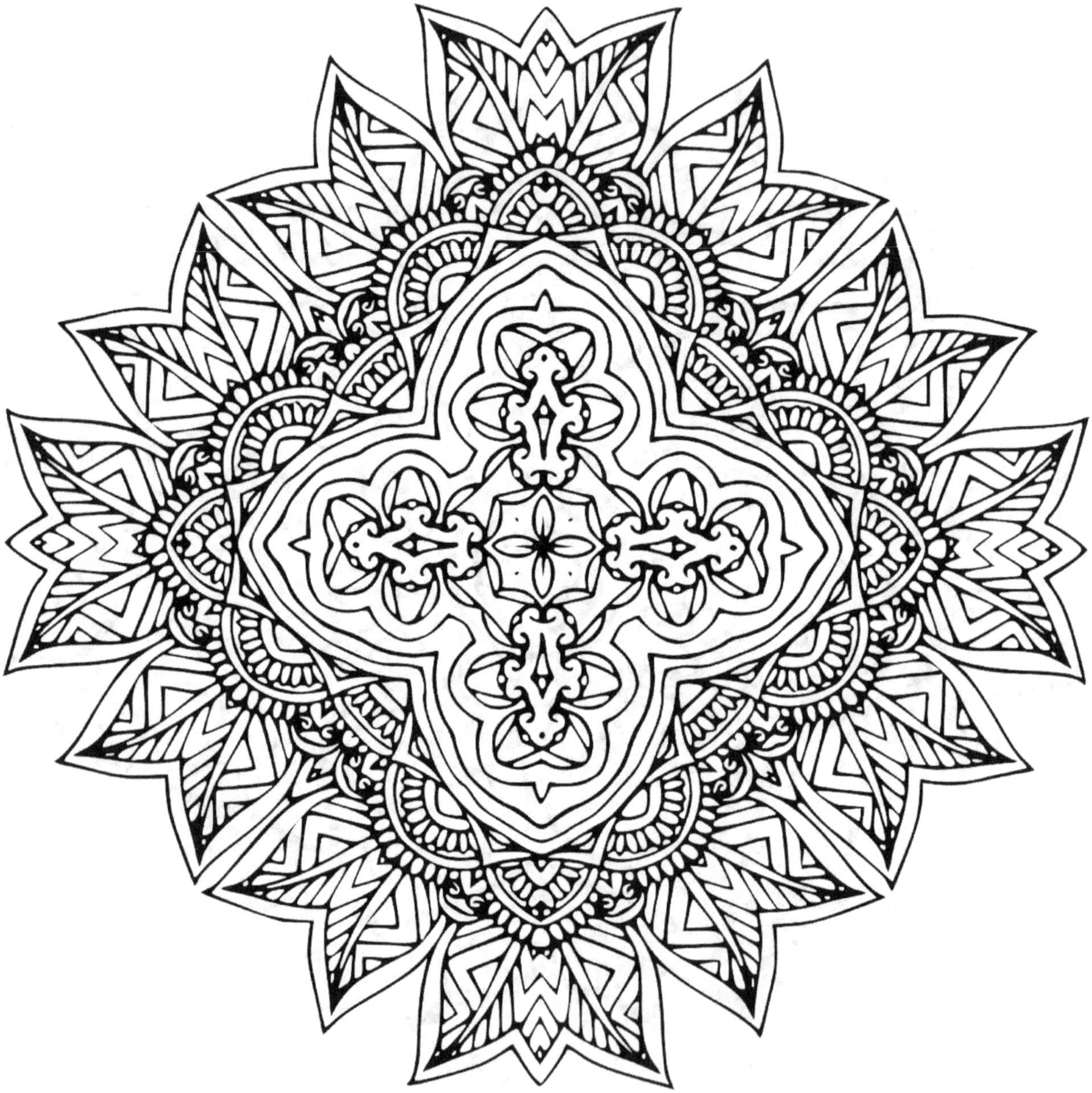

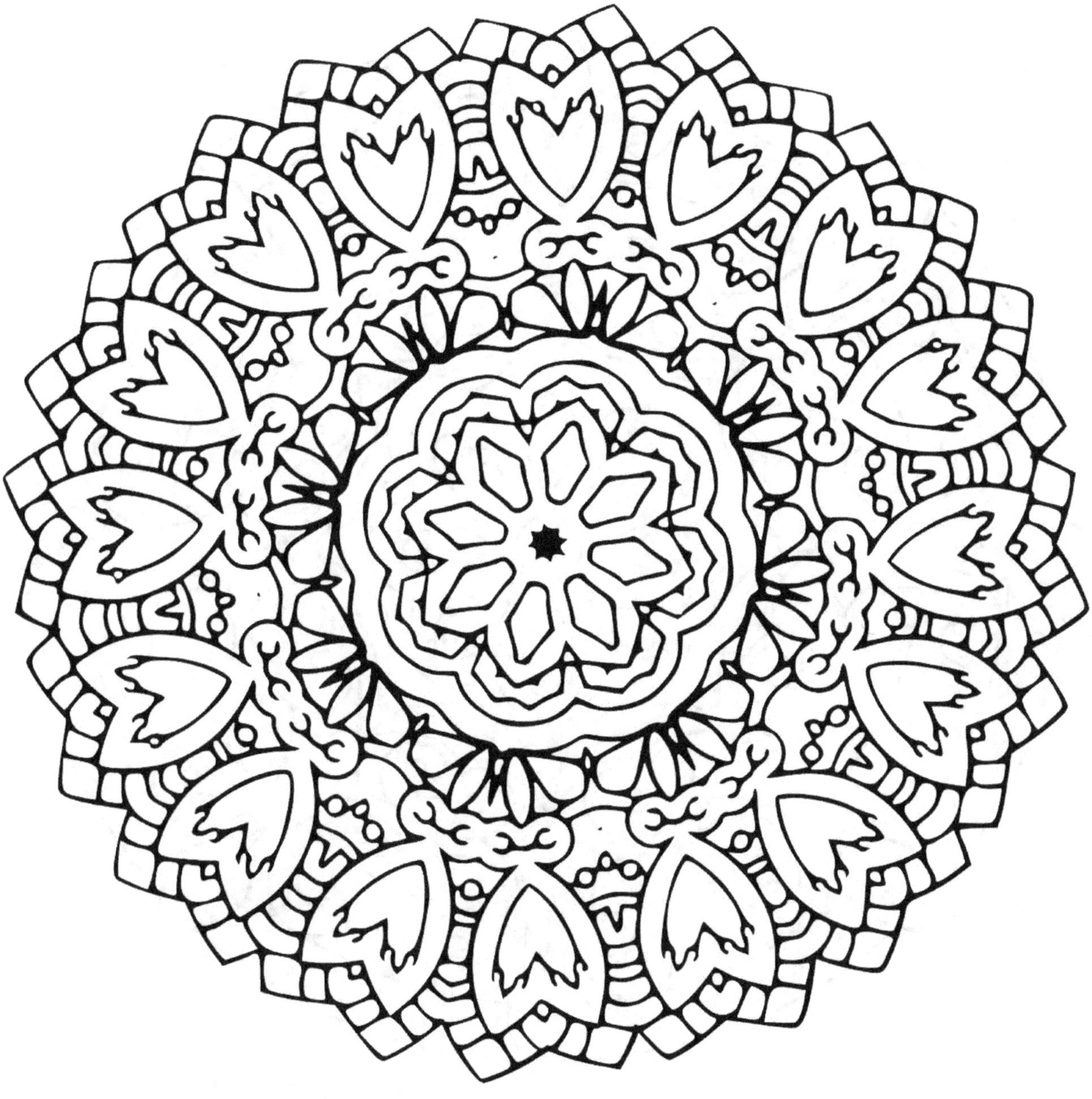

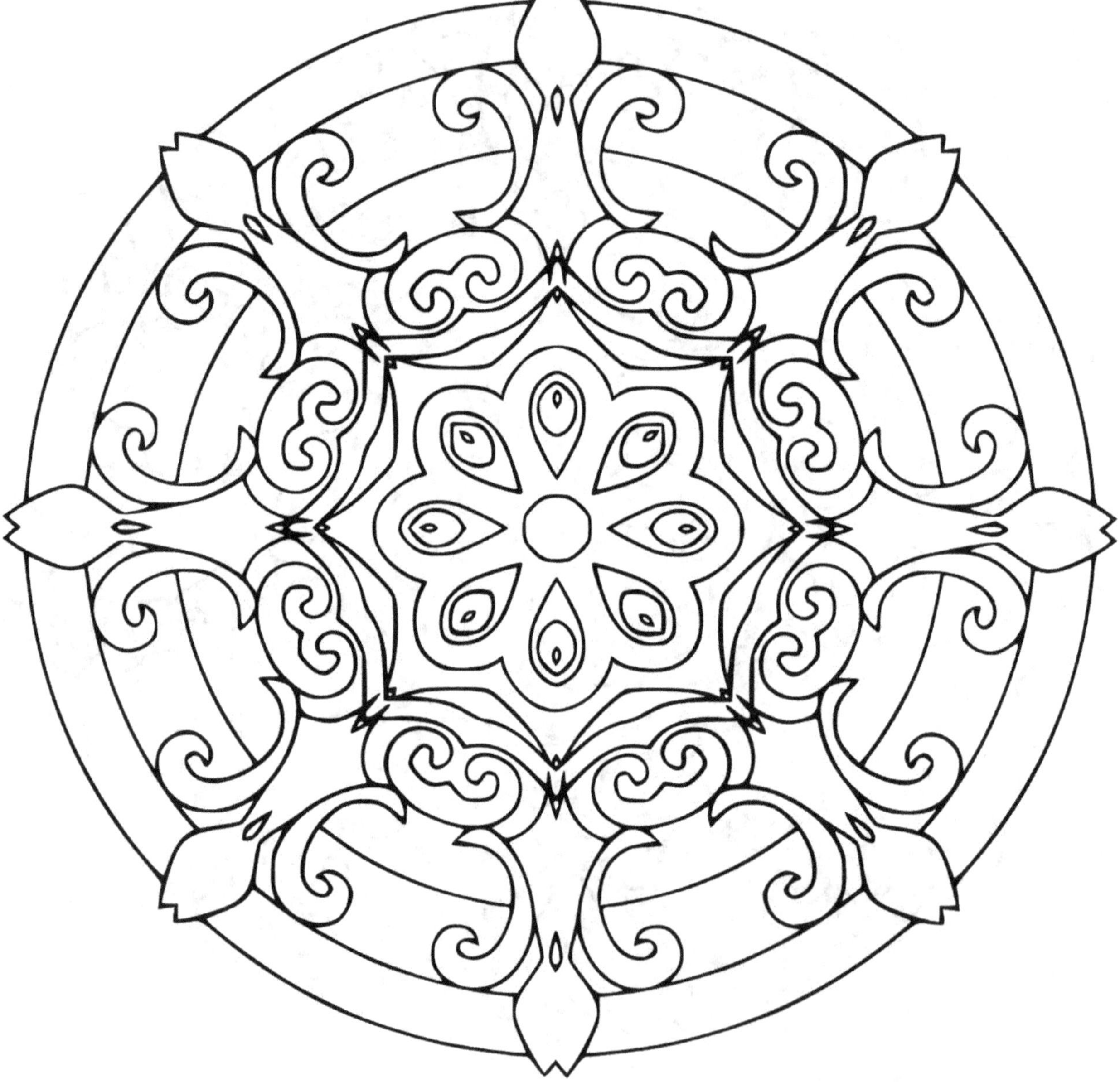

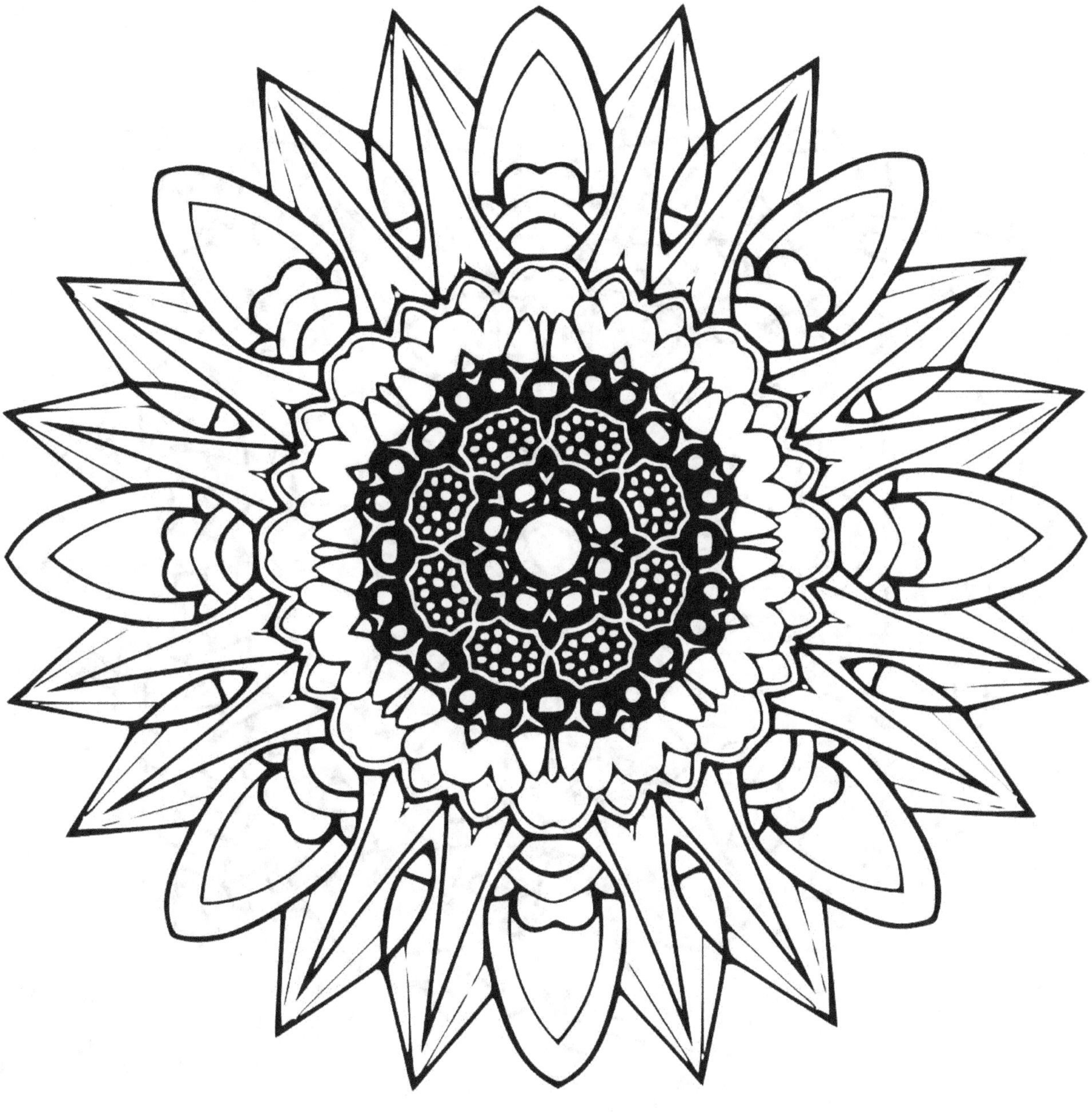

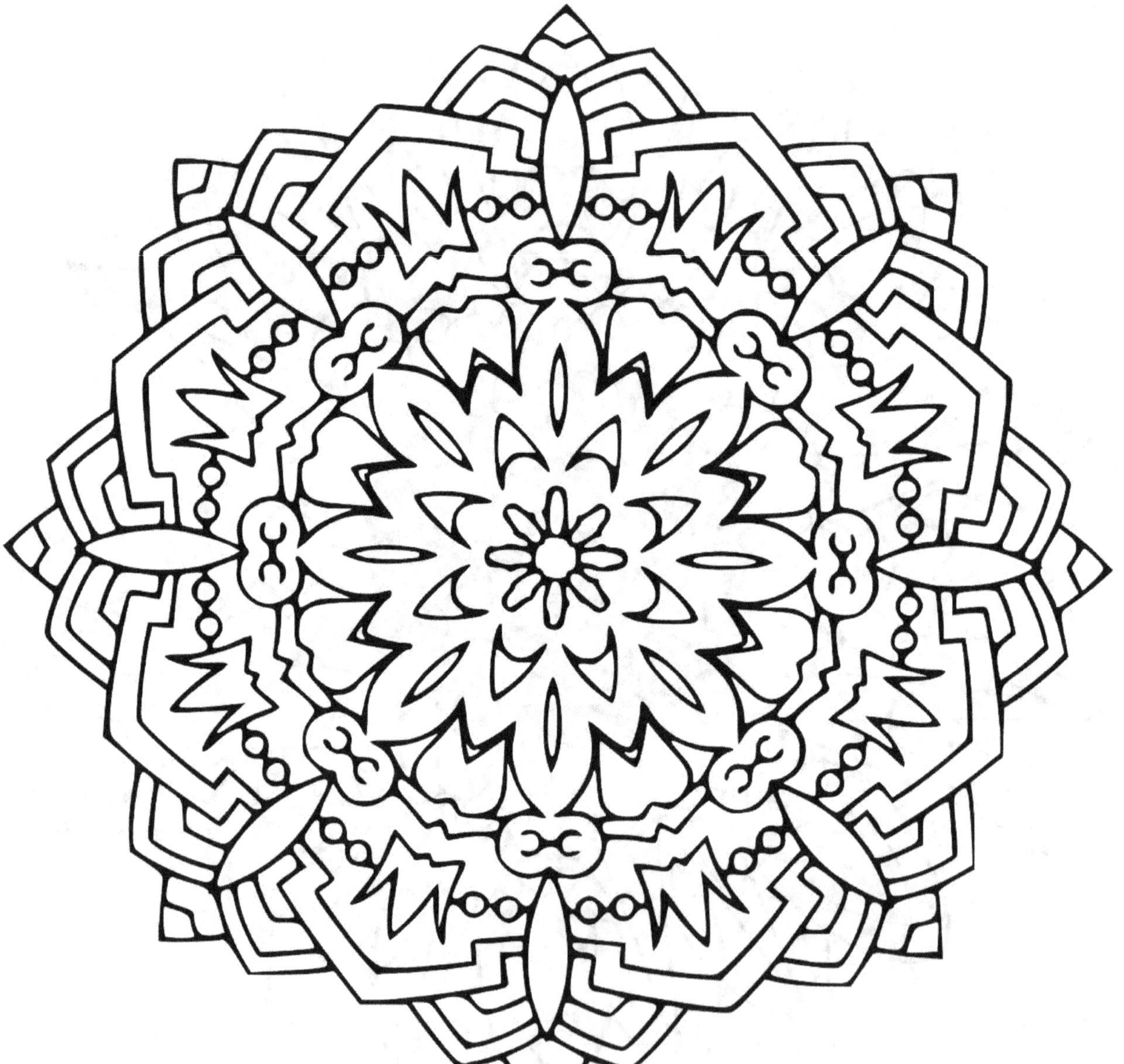

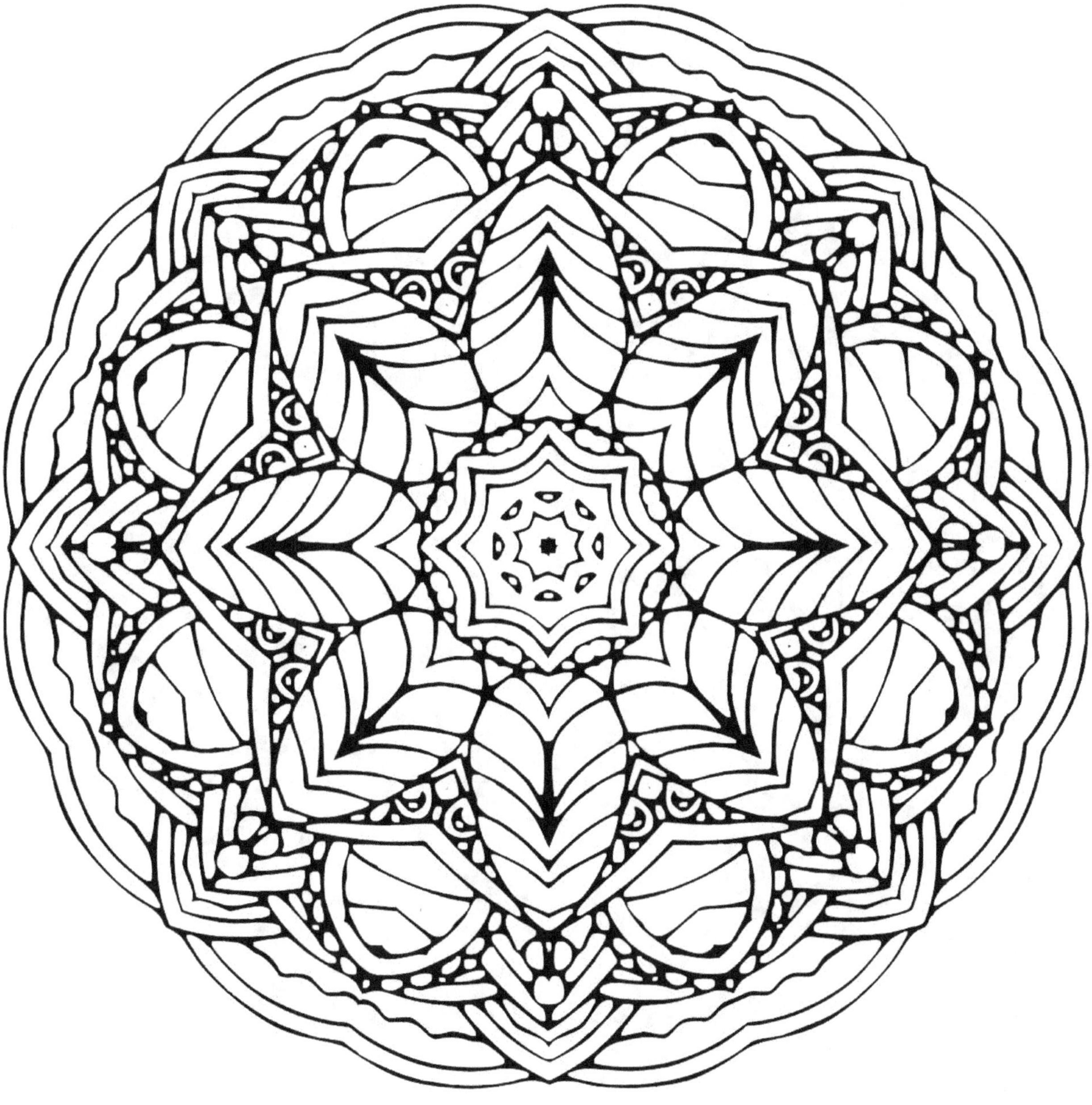

www.ingramcontent.com/pod-product-compliance
Lightning Source LLC
Chambersburg PA
CBHW081319180526
45170CB00007B/2773
* 9 7 8 1 5 4 4 8 7 8 5 3 9 *